And the Leaves said, "Change!"

Ashley Johnson

BookLeaf
Publishing

India | USA | UK

Presentation by *BookLeaf Publishing*

Web: www.bookleafpub.com

E-mail: info@bookleafpub.com

ISBN: 9789360947798

First edition 2024

ACKNOWLEDGEMENT

Writing these poems has been a labor of love, and I have a few people, without whom, this would've never happened.

First and foremost, I extend my deepest appreciation to my partner Jai. My love, thank you for seeing me and handing me a mirror to look at myself. You are my muse, a consistent source of inspiration and compassion. Her encouragement fueled my passion for poetry and propelled me forward during moments of doubt. Thank you for all the ways you showed up in true partnership (including offering "first dance" feedback and editing some of these poems for submission).

I am indebted to my family (Denise, Clinton, CJ, Christian) for their belief, understanding, and endless support. Their love has always been my anchor, grounding me in each creative (or personal) experiment. To my grandmother Gladys, thank you for believing in my writing and always cheering me on.

I extend my heartfelt thanks to my friends (Haley, Felicia, Tyrek, and Nubia), whose jokes and honesty brought joy to the process. Your feedback and enthusiasm helped shape these poems into their final form.

To my fellow poets, writers, and critics, thank you in advance for your invaluable guidance and constructive feedback. I am continually inspired by your passion for the written word.

Lastly, I want to express my profound gratitude to you, the reader. It is a choice to support someone's art and yet another choice to actively engage with it. Thank you for choosing this work to be a part of your story.

PREFACE

I love words. I love the ways they move, how they take up space on a page, how they can make it easier for someone to feel you. Words are connectors and bridges.

That said, I have not been able to confidently call myself a writer for over a decade. Despite my love for how words make me feel, the rigor of craft and the disruption of community that first gave me that title soured me towards poetry.

These poems are some of the first that I've written since I was a student. I say that to say these poems will reflect a different voice, one that I am learning to speak with. It is as raw as only something authentic can be with the wisdom only living leaves.

This collection was put together in less than a moon cycle as a part of a 21-day challenge. It may be unfinished, but because all great stories start somewhere, I'm considering this collection my re-membering how to be myself. I am remembering myself as a writer, as a poet, as a woman. It's a call home to pages that have served as both comfort and catalyst for meaningful growth and reflection in my life.

And the Leaves said, "Change!"

And the Leaves said, *"Change!"*

shut the fuck up when you hear love talking

As if I had any to spare.
Whispering willow wisdom to a nigga
who speaks at love instead of learning from it,
who can lose herself in the middle of a
conversation
about all that was
and all that is yet to be.
Me—
airpods in trying desperately to keep anyone
from seeing me cry in the park.

shut the fuck up when you hear love talking

My soothsaying cousins—
in their language, failing and unwavering mean
the same thing.
So the leaves warned,

shut the fuck up when you hear love talking

"Change!"

in a way, they'd be sure I wouldn't ignore.
A bough broke through my blues
I looked up at this tree—
arms outstretched in a hug
big enough to take your breath away, and for a
second
I swore I heard my auntie saying

shut the fuck up when you hear love talking

"It's time for a change".
Her voice riding the wave between the rhythm
of the wind and the beat.
So I squinted hard to hear her better.
And the Leaves said, *"Change!"*
And I felt a love I knew only my ancestors could
speak.
So I smiled,
And I sat down to listen to the Trees.

Things I Forget to Love

1. Mirrors.
2. Fear—
3. the thorns in beautiful blooms.
4. Fear—
5. the work to harvest a beautiful bloom.
6. Hard work and the lessons it leaves.
7. The leaves.
8. The trees.
9. Mirrors.
10. Being seen.
11. Seeing myself—
12. Happy is an expensive freedom.
13. Freedom.
14. Tilling the soil for new growth.
15. New growth
16. Growing pains

Growing Pains (Part One)

Birth is the last time you will be whole
We spend our lives learning to body
before we can learn to body we lose skin

Pain is the 1st thing we learn of body

We love to pieces
             in pieces

You never love the whole of someone
We shed too much skin

There are pieces of me lost
I don't know where they are or whom they
belong to

So I don't grow old
I grow young
I shed skin and start over defenseless

Every 7 years you claim your new body
I've been brand new 3 times this life
         I told my skin it didn't belong to me

Lumber Mill
(the comment section)

Some kinds of laughter echo
like the whirring of saws—
a cackle can peel back the bark
Leaving us in our rawest form
Timber or tinder
'Til all we feel is flame

people who delight in laughter born in
destruction
assemble in virtual mills
behind glowing screens several times a day
to sharpen tongues and feed their noise—
A cacophony of clicks

It starts with a comment but quickly spreads
 like
            like
                    like
                            a contagion—this fire

What makes a man if not his ability to make

fire and war on any plane?
    A) A strength made of breaking bones and
        birch
    B) The ability to craft words into weapons
    C) To turn nature into blaze stoked by the
        embers of shame, roaring defiantly.
    D) This kind of laughter—
        means an undoing.

and who is it this time?
Fresh tinder.

And what are we having for dinner?
New meat.

And what is a slaughter without the laughter?
An echo in the roaring lumber mill waiting for
the trees to fall.

Shady Palm

Dear God,
I worry that **SCARED**
     and **SACRED**

have much more in common,
than the peculiar placement of the consonant C

Tell me Father
Is it better to be loved or feared?

Wildfires
(Hurt People Hurt People)

*"The child who is not embraced by the village will
burn it down to feel its warmth"*
- African Proverb

Where should the lost go
after they have forgotten our names
and swallowed our smiles

here we are cold
children of wintered mothers
seeds taught to flower but never fruit
With hatred boiling
hot enough to burn flesh or
night or homes to feel again

a child tossed like rain
knows only her own raw flesh
its lonely forest—
fruit falling from anyone's tree,
breaking limbs on its way

We the new-born evergreens
Baring a legacy of burning all things in our path

We will extinguish
the tongue
            once born by blood, forgotten

The Truth is

there are many nights I'm afraid—
Fear isn't *thee* word
to describe how *hard* it can feel to love again
in the land of lawless loves—
You kill or be killed
Cold shoulder blades
Turned against your most tender truths
If we're this scared of being vulnerable
shouldn't we call heartbreak murder?

There are many ways to die while you're warm
and hide the living ghosts among us

People who have died
before they've lived to love,
bleed mistrust into the earth.
Even the trees refuse their fruit fall for anyone

Are we all so afraid of Love that we greet it with
a grieving smile?

That we launch our souls at it in defense?
Everyone's fighting and the night is velvet and
speechless—
wondering why war
feels safer than being seen

Growing Pains (Part Two)

You can't love the whole of someone while
they're falling apart—
There are pieces of me lost
I don't know where they are or whom they
belong to.

You'll spend a life learning what loss means
trying to find the pieces and their owners.

All people just re-membering to body,
Gift some of yourself.
share piece with a stranger
—shed skin and start over defenseless.
Before we can truly learn to body we lose skin

Parseltongue

Everyone hates
the snake, but at least he sheds
his skin, starts again

A Legacy of Giving (Seed)

Last night I gave her   *Safe*
the way we give away all things that aren't
ours—

Slow, with hesitation
the way my mother taught me
I imagine how *Safe* shows up for her

exhausted and overworked—
Bonnet on Eyes heavy with sleep and
disappointment

She whispers, "*I am tired, but I'm here.*"

A seed is planted.

The Work

Sometimes, in therapy I look for an easy W
        No breakthroughs or tears
        No discussions dissecting dreams
        No re-membering of the past—
        necromancy of my childhood

When my therapist tells me to practice grace—
I can't find it in my heart not to go hard
Them John Henry genes
I know that we shouldn't "should" when we're
doing the work
But the body keeps the score and I should be so
much further ahead
                An easy win
No revelations or journaling necessary
I wonder if that is even still doing the work if I
go easy on myself—

how will I know I'm growing? Doesn't pain
mean it's working?
The work sits heavy on my chest and in the
crevices of my eyelids
It's hard to care about work when people are
dying
Shouldn't it be easier?

I'm doing the work and I'm so tired—

I forgot to send that email and finish the project
that was due yesterday
                              An easy win
My ancestors are in my ears telling me I
shouldn't worry
I know that we shouldn't "should" when we're
doing the work–

But these John Henry genes deserve an easy win
So I should
 make movies of moments I smile,
practice grace and celebration
with every breath I share—

        a little gratitude for my OGs, the trees.

PTSD

Those who have lived through war never forget
They take with them each loss and every
battle—
they become war

Smiles made of fire and flight
Bearing bone as both
welcome and weapon
The loneliness chilling the skin How cold is the
body when it becomes corpse?

We are what is left--
Our breath, this music
Our names smoke and ash
Endless and unfading

Somehow we survived the war

a nigga turns 32 and lights a spliff to
celebrate—this survival

When I stop to admire the plants

When I stop to admire the plants
It is rarely at a park,
flower shop
or garden
the places the city allows flora to live or die
my eye is drawn to patches of green and brown—
In brick and asphalt

I watch for signs of life as I know it.
A breathing, a bleeding, a song or dance,
or something human

When I stop to admire the plants
sometimes all I see are weeds,
a dandelion showing the wind
just how carefree life could be

I think about the danger and damage they cause
close my fingers tight around the body before I
uproot it.

it's usually a weed

I stop to see the plants my city allows to live and
thrive
it's usually a weed
when I admire how determined they are to grow

I know that they must think we are weeds

Composting

Grief is a sea many of us hold slick
across the roofs of our mouths
blades
We spit at each other from its depths

Our words are wet with the regret
of a hundred yesterdays
still sorry for this bloodline and the last
that didn't learn its lesson

a father who couldn't be a husband—
a wife who loves the Jesus way—
Sometimes sacrifice,
Sometimes martyr.
Can't flower everywhere you're planted
branches on the family tree splinter in the skin

In the dirt of collective memory,
we are seeds of hope, buried—
where pain once reigned.
Our roots outstretched, like bloodlines—
fingers of time, we trace the lessons learned.

Like worms, we squirm through the layers of
remorse and regret, we re-mix
Seeking the light
with each sunrise, a rebirth

A new lifetime pushes through the grime,
The past smells ripe with rot but like beacons,
guiding our way,
There's some love still to be had in the soil

We sprout
a testament to the strength found in decay

Love (Flower)

In the quiet of dawn,
Love arrives

a seed carried on whispers of wind, nestled in
the fertile soil of two hearts.
a tender thing, this love, small and unassuming,
pregnant with the promise of growth.
it takes root in the soul, burrowing deep—

Love unwinds its delicate tendrils, reaching out
to touch each other
and dancing in the sunlight of shared moments.
A slow awakening, this blossoming—
a gradual unfurling of petals in the warmth of
mutual understanding.

To see and be seen
each glance, each touch, each whispered word
Fertile food feeding the flora,

As days turn into weeks and weeks into months,
the seed takes root,
sending hearts skyward, cloud talking with glee
this growth from seed to sapling, from bud to
bloom.

Pink

She lives in the realm where dreams soar on a
gentle breeze,
Equal parts sunrise and sunset
Love in its truest hue
It dances in the petals, flushes in the dawn,
She's a rosy embrace, a tender song
The warmth of a first night kiss in candlelight

In every tender moment, finds her space.
A whispered secret in the dancing flames
sweet as my favorite candy
Safe and safe and safe
The flower before it blooms into fruit

bloom in gardens, in skies above,
A testament to beauty, to life, to love.

Lineage

My ancestors, the trees who hold us tender even
in our final moments
Offering shelter without rent, branches spread.
In their shadow, I learn to bloom and grow,
roots echo ancient melodies
and I dance along free-er for being green.

My tears they cradle, in bark and in bough,
Each drop a promise to rise anew somehow,
reminding me of how we flower
Amidst the chaos, their guidance holds a holy
peace

Through the whooping winds and silent night,
Feeding me in secret, their bounty abundant,
from trunk to tree.

I honor my ancestors,
whose whispers of wisdom I can see
In the rustle of leaves and the gentle sway,
Their love keeps me whole, from night to day.

Changing Leaves

OH! Audacity of we   this **Black**—
daring to be beautiful.
Dandelions   they call weeds.

  always growing without permission

Audacity of we   this **Black**—
To be flowers bearing fruit in a graveyard.
What was once a seed, perhaps
Has grown into a forest.

  We don't die we multiply

        this **Black**—
What are these brown bodies
if not   the trees
Arms spread wide
life-giving
sometimes tired but   still here.

I, too, have been   unarmed,
in this re-membering
My limbs bruised   not broken,
but   still here.

  The audacity—
what else is this skin if not the changing of the leaves

Cousin Talk
(Hotboxing with the Trees)

I've been kiki-ing with the trees after trying for
months to learn their language—
the leaves falling.
and I still have so much to learn

the trees–
know of grief, growth, leaving and loss
They have bent and broken and been reborn in
the process
Felt pain to bear both flowers and fruit
Felt seen
been grounded
Been tinder and fire

Did you know they hate the word autumn?
    *"Humans always try to make meaning
      without any real connection."*

I nod and say,
"We hate to admit what we don't know."
And they respond,

  "Now, THAT should've been Newton's Law."

They laugh
I laugh,

branches shifting in the wind,
The leaves falling.
We sit in all that is slow,
all that changes from green to yellow, from
yellow to brown

I say, *"This is the good life."*
They say,

"When will you learn—
this is the only way to live?"

Sunday's Best
(Soul Food)

Incantations and curses fill the belly with love—
That slide off the bone goodness
My ancestors talking round table
over a hot meal.
It's Sunday's best when they gather—
full of flavor and tongues.

Some of them wear worry like a glove
what to do and what to do and what to do
                        between chews

Slinging questions
*"Why don't she just walk the road we laid out for
her?!"*
A cacophony of kissed teeth and "Mhms"
                        between chews

Yelling at cosmic movie screen
We spoke of slowing, not halting altogether
what to do and what to do and what to do
                        between chews
They slide a plate of
patience and guidance,
a gentle nudge forward.
Food for the soul
to be eaten slow.

Love (Fruit)

It is in the quiet moments I think most about how I
have been most transformed by Love
I revel in the alchemy,
Beaming in all that feels new

In its gentle embrace, I Kundalini
shed the skin of my former self,
Emerging, fragile and fierce, softer than I've ever
been

As if a relentless sculptor, shaping me with tender
hands,
Carved away the rough edges, smoothing the
jagged contours.
Each caress a sacred syllable, spelling out my
destiny.

I am no longer the same as I once was,
Love has etched its story upon my soul.
Woven into my skin an essence so sweet
Some flowers are jealous of me
In its presence, I am both grounded and weightless,
A breeze, through the trees on a journey of
becoming–
Love tilled itself into the fabric of my being,
and it is my gift to grow and plant new seeds.

Harvest

The sweetest fruit is the one
we worked hardest for
a labor of love and lust

Your "*almost…*—
a delicate flower
each touch blossoms a new beginning,
each kiss a birth of longing deep—
roots entwined,
Bodies be the most beautiful trees

Skin a canvas of rich earth
Sun-kissed
Your "*I'm close…*—

Winds whispering wet along the blades of grass
My tongue sways and sighs, praying for rain

My fingers dance upon your fertile ground,
In each caress, your storm draws near,
Torrents of pleasure pouring down,
Each raindrop a tremor, a tempest-tossed.
Until finally, the storm finds release,

Echoes of thunder—
In passion's sound, the soil is tilled,
A steady hand, keeping desires fulfilled.

In this garden, love finds its space.

Its bounty ripe,
our roots embrace, and we merge as one.
Honeydew in our flowers

a labor of love and lust

Our proud smile warming the spot
where soil and skin in rapture met—
our harvest yields fruit, forever sweet.